Corned Beef On Lies

Corned Beef On Lies

The Laugh Track From My 83-Year Life Trek

by Gloria Krasnow Liebenson
Illustrations—Shayna Sara Skolnik

iUniverse, Inc.
New York Lincoln Shanghai

Corned Beef On Lies
The Laugh Track From My 83-Year Life Trek

Copyright © 2005 by Gloria Krasnow Liebenson

iUniverse books may be ordered through booksellers or by contacting:

iUniverse
2021 Pine Lake Road, Suite 100
Lincoln, NE 68512
www.iuniverse.com
1-800-Authors (1-800-288-4677)

Text and Title by Gloria Krasnow Liebenson © 2005
Illustrations by Shayna Sara Skolnik © 2005
Book Design and Back Cover Photographs by F. Borden Mace © 2005
Library of Congress Control Number: 2005901973

ISBN-13: 978-0-595-35997-4 (pbk)
ISBN-13: 978-0-595-80845-8 (cloth)
ISBN-13: 978-0-595-80448-1 (ebk)
ISBN-10: 0-595-35997-3 (pbk)
ISBN-10: 0-595-80845-X (cloth)
ISBN-10: 0-595-80448-9 (ebk)

Printed in the United States of America

"I Count Only the Sunny Hours" *
William Hazlett 1778–1830

(Written on a Sundial near Venice, Italy)

*for the most part

Preface

This is a collection of "remember-when" stories—mostly funny. If you find a few tears among the chuckles, and giggles and guffaws, well, that's life, isn't it?

In Memory of My High School English Teacher

Miss Ella Wilhelmina Magdalena Kracke

Contents

Gloria Krasnow Liebenson

The Brain in My Behind

The year was 1928. Teddy was ten and Bobby was twelve. We were living in an apartment at Van Buren and Crawford in Chicago, Illinois.

Nineteen twenty-eight. Six years old. No more frivolous kindergarten nonsense. No! No more time to waste on kid stuff. Mere days to meet the prerequisite for first grade, and the troops were at a standstill. My education was on hold until I could demonstrate that I could print my name.

Therein lies my tale. (More to the point—my tail.) The name-printing project picked up in intensity one afternoon when Mama—lugging a bulky package—climbed the steps leading to our third-floor apartment. She proceeded to unwrap one of those easel-type blackboards and to set it up in the bedroom shared by Bobby and Teddy. She popped open a small box of white chalk and positioned two sticks in the groove beneath the slate.

Bobby was in the living room, where he had settled into the sofa to hear a season-opener baseball game. Mama clicked off the radio and said, "Take your sister into the bedroom and stay there with her until she learns how to print her name." You see, Mama was now at her wits' end. She had only recently resigned herself to my unalterable left-handedness, but she was stymied by an unexpected by-product of that "affliction," which caused GLORIA KRASNOW to appear on paper as AIROLG WONSARK whenever I attempted to print my name. Trust me. I tried. I tried and tried again, but it was the same every time.

And every one of those times, Mama—a palm spread over her ample bosom—would release a deep sigh.

Bobby, though visibly disinclined to do so, rose from the sofa. I followed him into the bedroom. He picked up a piece of chalk and handed a second one to me. He printed my name in really big letters—so big that my name nearly filled half of the slate. He printed GLORIA KRASNOW. Then he sat down, his long, skinny legs dangling from the foot of the bed. He said, "Now, you write exactly what I wrote." I stood facing the blackboard and I printed AIROLG WONSARK. I stood back and studied my handiwork; it looked perfectly fine to me.

But not so Bobby. His lips were pressed together and his face was red. He jumped from the bed and ran from the room, slamming the door behind him. I could hear him talking to Mama who was in the kitchen preparing dinner. I fell back onto the bed crying as I listened to Bobby. "I give up. She's just a plain dummy and she's always gonna be a dummy."

Mama's voice was loud. "Don't you dare call your sister a dummy. Don't you dare! That child has more brain in her behind than you have in your head!"

I was stunned and I proceeded to process this valuable new information—Eureka! That was it! I did have a brain after all. How could I have been smart with my fingers when I had never even known where my brain was? To you, perhaps, this reasoning may seem somewhat bizarre, but I assure you it made perfect sense within the parameters of my literal six-year-old intellect.

Fast forward 24 hours. Little Gloria is home with the cleaning lady and the doorbell sounds. Enter my best-friend-of-the-week, Ramona Schimmelfarb (not her real name, but not that far from her real name). She asks: "Can you play?" Ramona—this is a critical element of my story—was the only-child, prized, protected offspring of parents who had anointed me her playmate only after ascertaining that ours was a respectable household headed by a doctor daddy. I had already bestowed upon her the best-friend privilege of sharing my good news (the blackboard) as well as my bad news (the name-writing malfunction).

Ramona skipped into my brothers' bedroom, swept up a stick of chalk and with (which I still consider undue flourish) cut a white swath across the width of the slate: RAMONA SCHIMMELFARB (Actually, she printed her real name.) and stepped back to admire her artistry. Then what did she do? In a gesture of feline cunning well beyond her six years, she placed the chalk in my hand and said, "Now you."

I was ready for her. "Well, Smarty, it just so happens that I could write better than anyone, but I don't write the same as anyone. My brain is in my behind."

"Oh yeah?" said Ramona. "Betcha can't prove it."

"Can too," I said. "I'm gonna put a pencil in here (pointing to my rear) and I'm gonna write my name on the floor." That grabbed Ramona's attention.

I found an eraser-tipped pencil in the desk drawer, lowered my panties and introduced the pencil into this unaccustomed venue. Alas! When I squatted on my haunches to prove my point, the pencil tracks were indistinguishable on the varnished bedroom floor. Practical, serious Ramona reasoned that the white tile bathroom floor might provide a better writing surface. In addition, she was warming to the whole project and found her own pencil so that she could test the literacy of her behind.

The experiment was a partial success in terms of leaving our imprints on the bathroom floor, but we were soon bored with the project and settled into more traditional play until it was time for Ramona to leave.

Now, bear with me as we fast-forward once again—this time to approximately nine o'clock that evening. I was asleep and had not heard the doorbell. Papa shook me awake gently. "Gloria," he said, "put on your robe and come into the living room." Barely awake, I faced, in the living room: Mama seated and wearing her good maroon dress (the one with the white lace collar) and facing two strange grownups. "Gloria," she said, "these are Ramona's parents." Puzzled and still sleep-dazed, I smiled politely and sat down facing our guests.

Then, Papa spoke. "Ramona told her parents that something bad happened here today and now, we want to ask you about it."

"Nothing happened, Papa. We played and then Ramona had to go home."

Ramona's father was not smiling. "We asked Ramona if she had fun here today and she told us that you closed yourselves into the lavatory and placed pencils into your private parts. We would like to know why you did that and we would like to know who taught you to do that. Ramona's mother and I are not happy about this."

Mama and Papa were staring at me. I said, "Well, I was the only one who needed to do that, but Ramona said she wanted to, so I let her."

Mama's mouth fell open. "You needed to do that? You needed to do what?"

I said, "Remember, Mama, how you said that my brain is in my behind? And how I need to learn to print my name the right way? I was trying to find out if my behind could print my name the way it's supposed to be."

Nobody said anything for a really long time. I wasn't sure about what I should say next or maybe just go back to bed. Finally, Papa said, "Gloria, it's very late. Go to bed now."

My best friend right after that was a girl named Minerva Shinitsky (her real name).

Mama Takes Credit

The year was 1929 and we were still living in the apartment at Van Buren and Crawford. I loved my Saturdays in those days because Saturday meant having Mama all to myself for most of the day. It was the day for making our rounds: Osnoss Bakery on South Crawford for hot rolls and my complimentary sugar cookie; the "drygoods" store for notions; the "fruit" store for produce and finally, the butcher shop for ("Please, Mama, lamb chops!") usually, lamb chops.

On a particular Saturday morning, however, we diverted from this pleasant routine, taking a detour that led us further than anyone could have predicted. We took a detour that led us to a new-fangled concept called Credit.

It was the Saturday we boarded a streetcar that took us to Hartman's Furniture and Carpet Store. When we made our way out of the streetcar, Mama didn't go into the store right away. She stood at the store window transfixed—peering through the glass at every curlicue and knob of a "French" bedroom grouping—a style all the rage in the '20's.

Mama motioned me to follow her into the store, where, as one might expect, a jovial salesman welcomed us. We stood all of us in spirited admiration of the total "suite": chiffonier for Papa, dresser for Mama, a night stand for each and (After all, this was the "moderne" 1920's.) twin beds to complete the ensemble.

Mama's smile faded when the smiley salesman quoted the price for all of this splendor. Mama touched my elbow and nodded in the direction of the exit.

"Ma'am," the salesman said, "please don't let the price stand in your way. There's a very easy way for you to enjoy this beautiful furniture without putting out a lot of money. It's called Buying on Credit." Credit. It had a nice ring to it....

"All you need to pay is a very small down payment." Mama asked howthat could be. He was eager to explain. After that modest down payment, all Mama needed to do was to make a small payment before the 15th of every month until, before many months had passed, she would own the furniture free and clear. Credit! What a wonderful new idea! America! America, the Golden Land.

So, that is how it came to pass that Mama and Papa acquired their elegant French bedroom suite. But wait! Who knew that 1929 was destined to become Year One of The Great Depression? Pretty soon, those 15ths rolled around faster and faster—and poor Mama. She loved her new furniture, but the stress generated by this novel method of doing business, was almost too much for her. Around the 10th of every month, we would find Mama in a blue funk, bemoaning the possibility that she couldn't meet that month's furniture payment. By the 12th of the month, dread set it. She was certain that Hartman's would come for her treasured furniture on the 15th.

(Somehow, after a long, long time, the furniture was paid for.)

Now, Mr. and Mrs. P. enter the picture. They were old friends of Mama and Papa. In fact, Mrs. P. and Mama shared a common history of birthplace and emigration to America. In one important aspect, however, they parted ways. Mr. P., a wholesaler of tobacco products, had amassed a sizable fortune—hence, was able to provide his family with a lifestyle light-years beyond anything our family could aspire to. They lived—even in those grey

Depression days—a life of privilege. Grand tours to faraway places, a Packard automobile, a driver, costly clothing, opulent decor. When Mrs. P. would return from Paris with those little gift vials of Evening in Paris perfume, Mama's gratitude was bittersweet.

Every now and then, our family would be invited to the P.'s for Sunday dinner. Not often, but sometimes. On one of those occasions—soon after the P.'s had returned from one of their European jaunts-Mama noticed an end table she had not seen before.

Mama commented, "That's a lovely table. Is it new?"

Mrs. P. pursed her lips. "Margaret," she said, "of course that 's not new. Actually, it goes back to Louis the Sixteenth."

Mama didn't miss a beat. "And, actually I have a whole room full of furniture that goes back to Hartman's the fifteenth."

Maxwell Street Memoirs

Mama hated sweaters. I'm not sure exactly why. It could have been that she was vain about adding bulk to her well-rounded upper arms. I only know that she hated sweaters so much that even a sweater-clad stranger was fair game. "Look at that woman! She looks like King Levinsky's sister!"

Who was King Levinsky? Who was King Levinsky's sister? Who cared? Mama had only to say her name and we children would dissolve into paroxysms of laughter. It just sounded so funny.

Eventually, when Teddy and Bobby grew a bit older and discovered the sports pages of the Chicago Tribune, we learned that King Levinsky was a well-known heavyweight boxer during the 1920's and into the '30's. The way Mama told it, his full-bodied sister wore her trademark heavy sweater while wheeling and dealing at the entrance to her thriving fish stand on Maxwell Street.

I was a little girl then and I loved the noise and bustle of that vibrant ghetto. On Sundays, I would beg Papa to take me there (Mama would have none of that.) to see the pushcart peddlers and listen to the merchants hawking their wares at the entrances to their stores. Alas, that Maxwell Street is no more. I know that because on December 1st, 1998 I spotted, in the The Washington Post, a story written by Kari Lyderson: "Maxwell Street Farewell Blues—A Slice of Bygone Chicago Faces the Developer's Ax."

Lyderson's story evoked in me a flood of nearly lost memories. King Levinsky's sister, for sure, but more importantly—Papa and Maxwell Street.

Papa was Henry Randolph Krasnow, M.D. I think you'll agree the name has a nice ring to it. Dignified. That described Papa. Military bearing. One of the last holdouts to surrender those unyielding detachable shirt collars. From whence came the name? Well, the Henry part must have evolved out of Harris—the name on the copy of the ship's manifest which my cousin, Leslie Saxon shared with me. Krasnow? Obviously an Anglicisation of Krasnoff or Krasnofsky. However, the Randolph part is a mystery; I think Papa just liked the sound of it.

Papa was born in Russia—in Odessa, a city renowned for its rich culture. He arrived in America in the early 1900's when he was twenty-three years old. He was poor but well grounded in music and literature. As was customary during that period of heavy immigration, he was accompanied by his father and some of his siblings, with the expectation that additional family members would follow.

Mama and Papa spoke little about their early lives in Czarist Russia, but over the years, I did learn that Papa had been a nurse in Russia, and had supplemented his income (meanwhile nurturing his passion for music) by working as a "claque". (Claques were young people who—planted strategically in a concert hall or opera house—were paid to clap at preordained parts of the performance.)

Those first emigrated Krasnows and the family members who followed them, settled in Springfield, Massachusetts and in New Haven, Connecticut. Papa—eldest of the siblings—was drawn to New York City, where his livelihood came from a diversity of jobs: court translator of Russian to English, (He had a facility for languages.) sparring partner in a gym and eventually, minor roles on the stage. It was in the theater that he was befriended by a fatherly old man who urged Papa to reassess his scattered lifestyle and focus on his initial interest in Medicine—ideally making a fresh start distanced from the distractions of New York City.

And that's how Papa found himself in Valparaiso, Indiana, the home of Valparaiso University which was reputed to welcome immigrants. After he had earned a pre-medical degree, he gravitated to Chicago and Rush Medical College. It was during his internship at the American Hospital in Chicago (continuing to supplement his income by tutoring) that he was introduced to Mama, a recent immigrant from Kiev. She was employed as a nurse at the Cook County Hospital and eager to learn the English language. They married after a brief courtship and Papa set up his practice at Halsted and Maxwell.

Maxwell Street early in the 20th Century bore a close resemblance to those bazaars and street markets which our generation finds so picturesque when we visit foreign countries. Among Maxwell Street's ethnic mix of immigrant pushcart peddlers and street vendors, there was a sizeable concentration of newly-arrived Russians, for whom Papa—the very first Russian-speaking physician to practice in Chicago—served as an unofficial clearinghouse. Confronted with what must have seemed an overwhelmingly confusing city environment, those people would turn to Papa for information and contacts.

Jane Addams' Hull House, a settlement house dubbed the "Cathedral of Humanity" was located on Halsted Street, close to Papa's office. Hull House was famous back then for its commitment to support services for people of all ages and ethnicities. Papa was befriended by Jane Addams and she enlisted his aid in some of her settlement house projects.

Eventually, some years before I was born, Papa and Mama vacated that teeming neighborhood for a more "residential" atmosphere.

Another almost-faded Maxwell Street memory embodies an establishment that I think was called the Café Royale. I recall Papa taking me there perhaps twice or three times when I was about six years old. I remember a crowded, smoky room where bearded men drank tea from glasses caged in filigreed metal holders. Arguments about who-knows-what grew increasingly vociferous as the evening wore on, while in the background one could hear lively Russian music. I loved it. When I asked Papa to take me there again, Mama put her foot down. Apparently, she took a dim view of "those Muzhiki".

Papa's patients and friends were mostly from the world of music and theater, and those were the people who filled our home with music and lively conversation. However, much to Mama's distress, Papa's total lack of business acumen coupled with the Great Depression, yielded a scarcity of worldly goods. On the other hand, we children were privy to a precious legacy of cultural enrichment, which I guess, in retrospect, was not too shabby of an inheritance.

The Doodle Bug

The year was 1932. I was ten years old. Teddy was fourteen. We lived at Central and Quincy. That's how people would tell you where they lived. Van Buren and Crawford, Washington and Pine, Leland and Clarendon. And, if you happened to live in a building in the middle of the block? Didn't matter. Just tell me your intersection. Why? I haven't a clue.

Nineteen Thirty-Two. A year when Depression (not today's lower-case clinical variety) ruled. We ate, drank, breathed—nay, were virtually suffocated by Depression. Picture it: the 1930's. Long before the advent of home television. Long before anything remotely resembling today's electronic amusements. Actually, not too long after the phenomenon of radio. But first and foremost, far removed from any kid fun that called for the expenditure of money.

Hence, once it was determined that the weather outside was too hot or too cold for a game of kick-the-can or a picnic in Columbus Park, fun for me was wherever my fertile ten-year-old imagination happened to light. So that's how it happened that on one particular summer day, fun popped up in the form of a fat, floppy drapery tassel which, in another life, had girdled a satiny side-panel, the likes of which disappeared after "moderne" Venetian blinds were discovered by motion picture set designers and—as follows the night the day—showed up in home decor. The once-so-omnipresent billowy, floor-puddling "hangings" were cast aside, along with their tassled tiebacks.

I studied my new find. I wiggled it over the dining room table, studying the tendrils that fanned out from its slender tubular spool to dissolve into a quivering mass of silken worms.

Remember, I was only ten. Old enough to sense delicious possibilities but clearly in need of my brother's older, wiser head. Plus, of course, his future value for the blame-shifting that is the God-given right of every last-born. I went out to the porch to summon Teddy. Another digression: In the little piece of Chicago where I dwelt, all exterior spaces which were components of dwellings, were called porches. Terraces? Verandas? Balconies? Patios? Forget it!

Our particular "porch" was actually a metal-fenced, narrow concrete-floored balcony, accessible from the living room of our third-floor apartment and adjacent to the balcony of our across-the-hall neighbors. The balcony, you see, serves as a backdrop for the crime unfolding.

I found Teddy napping on what we referred to euphemistically as our steamer chair. Though it pained me to awaken him, Mama was due home with the groceries momentarily; time was of the essence.

You need to understand about Teddy. He was a brother you could count on. The brother I could trust with my cache of forbidden Fourth of July fireworks. The brother whose long arms could reach the top shelf of the cabinet where Mama hid the candy. The brother who knew where Mama hid the key to the locked radio console. I knew whom I was dealing with.

I shook Teddy awake. He rolled off of the canvas strip seat onto the concrete floor, picked himself up and followed me indoors. I pointed to my find and said, "Teddy, what is this?" He said, "What is this? It's a Doodle Bug." I always knew that Teddy was smart, but in this instance, he was brilliant. The diabolical plot that ensued, proved to satisfy all three dictionary definitions of Doodle Bug:

1. An insect

2. A divining rod

3. To waste time

Teddy appreciated the urgency of our situation. "Okay," he said, "don't ask me any questions. Bring me scissors and a spool of heavy black coat thread from Mama's sewing box (actually a small tin box—Mama was not your major seamstress) and hurry!" I rushed to comply.

Teddy sat down and proceeded to fabricate the drapery tassel into—as I would soon learn—an instrument of terror. First, he cut off about one foot of thread, which he fastened firmly around the neck of the tassel. (Did I mention? There was a Boy Scout knot-tying badge on his bedroom wall.) He attached the dangling thread end to the thread end of the spool. Then, he said, "It needs to be dark outside but not pitch dark, for this to work. Hide it good and I'll show you about it tonight." Our timing was perfect; just then, Mama rang the doorbell.

Now, it is five or six hours later. Dinner dishes dried and put away. Family seated in the living room, tuned in to The Goldbergs. (Remember? "Yoo Hoo, Mrs. Bloom". Trust me. It was a classic.) Teddy, seated next to me on the sofa, elbows my ribs and jerks his head conspiratorially in the direction of the balcony. He rises slowly, opens the balcony door and exits. Shortly thereafter, I rise as well and go to retrieve the Doodle Bug from the depths of my underwear drawer and join Teddy on the balcony.

At this point, I need to explain the setting. That building we lived in at Central and Quincy was—on the Central Avenue side—a large three-story walkup. Where it turned the corner to become a courtyard complex on the Quincy side, there was Hilner's Delicatessen. Actually the neighborhood was residential, but as was the case in many such neighborhoods, there was a sole convenience store planted at ground level for an emergency quarter-pound of butter or quart of milk—or for that nectar of the gods—a chocolate "phoss". (I think that was the Chicago version of New York's two-cents-plain but with an added spritz of chocolate sauce.)

Evenings, when Hilner's seemed to be busiest, departing shoppers, laden with their brown paper sacks, tended to step cautiously because outdoor lighting was limited to the reflection of the store lights, plus two ornamental sidelights at our building entrance and the dim, old-fashioned street lamp standing between the two. I dwell upon the lighting only because that is what inspired Teddy in the crafting of his plot.

That evening, conditions were ideal. It was dusk. Just dark enough for the lights to be lit, just as Teddy had specified earlier, not pitch dark.

Furtively, we checked the glass balcony door. Good! The family was still in the grip of the Goldbergs.

Teddy leaned over the balcony railing, unwound the spool and jiggled the Doodle Bug until it rested precisely in front of our building's entrance door—between the two sidelights and as closely as he could manage, at head height. The black thread, of course, blended into the darkness and the Doodle Bug was discernable only as a monstrous flying—a monstrous flying <u>what</u>? This was just too good. We were overcome with fits of laughter as we waited eagerly for our first victim to exit Hilner's—preferably carrying a really big bag of groceries. We craned our necks over the railing, our eyes glued to Hilner's door. And, finally—Wow! Not one, but two women, both struggling with armsful of grocery bags and look! They're heading down Central!

My brother's lifelong propensity for attention to detail served him well now. With exquisite timing, he held the Doodle Bug as motionless as the mild breeze would permit. Then, exactly when the shoppers were aligned with our building door, he pumped the Doodle Bug up and down wildly, sending the tendrils flying crazily in all directions.

Pandemonium set in. The two women shrieked—one of them ignoring the sack that fell to the sidewalk. They turned and fled back into Hilner's with (we later learned) hysterical accounts of a monstrous flying creature "not an insect, not a bird and I swear on my mother's grave, <u>this big</u>!" The store emptied. Teddy and I crouched on the concrete floor, watching in terror as a posse formed—its recruits fanning out to track down this creature from hell.

My brother and I crept back into the living room, standing erect again just as Mama was turning to us. "How is it outside?" she asked. "I think I'll sit out for a while."

"Mama," I said, "it's nice outside but people are yelling about some crazy flying creature let loose. Wait a little while."

Sex Ed Circa 1932

In retrospect, it seems to me that for most of my early childhood, I was consumed by two questions: (1) How do babies get into ladies' stomachs? and (2) How do babies get out of ladies' stomachs?

I must have been eight or nine when I asked Mama how I could get a baby for myself. She explained that God doesn't give a baby to an unmarried lady because He wants to make sure that there is a papa who is working and able to support the baby.

Before I even had an opportunity to weigh the logic in that story, the newspapers were emblazoned with screaming headlines (Remember: "Extry, Extry—Extry Paper!") declaring that unmarried film star Marion Davies gave birth to a baby fathered by William Randolph Hearst.

"Mama," I said, "how come God gave her a baby?"

As always, Mama was quick on the uptake. "God already knew that Marion Davies had enough money to support a baby."

But do you know what? By that time, I was growing suspicious.

The second part of my dilemma—how do babies get out of a lady's stomach?—was solved to my satisfaction after consultation with my best friend Ruthie. We both agreed that since the baby was inside of the stomach (and since we couldn't figure any other earthly use for a belly button) the belly button must expand for the baby to pop out. Made sense.

Until! Until on a summer Saturday in 1933. I was eleven years old, waiting outside of our neighborhood movie theater for my best friend Ruthie. Standing nearby was my classmate Gerald waiting for his boyfriend Marvin.

Gerald greeted me saying, "Hey, dya wanna hear a really good joke I just heard?" Even then, I was always ready for a really good joke. "Yeah," I said, "sure."

Gerald said, "Old Nick stuck his Tootsie Roll into Fat Emma's Milky Way and out came Baby Ruth."

Case closed.

Hebrew Lesson

The year was 1934. I was twelve years old, enrolled in the seventh grade at the Robert Emmet School in Chicago. Typical of most Depression-era neighborhood schools, Emmet averaged 50 to 60 pupils per class, and, per class, a weary teacher scraping along on perennially late paychecks. There were no school buses—no need for them because in that tightly-packed neighbor-hood, a student was likely to live within a few blocks of the school.

In my seventh grade class, however, there was one exception in the person of a boy I identify as J.P. (I am withholding his name considering the possibility that he grew up to be a really nice person, but I am not holding my breath.) J.P. lived a whole mile away, but had been granted special dispensation to attend Emmet, we were told, because he had a relative teaching there.

J.P. was a wiry, bespectacled boy with curly blond hair. His clothing was immaculate. Every morning, he arrived wearing a freshly laundered starched white shirt. His hand flew up in response to every one of Teacher's questions. His feet were fleet at the very suggestion of Teacher's errands. His prize-winning Palmer Method handwriting enhanced his smudge-free compositions. His manners were beautiful. None of us—we, his classmates—knew quite what to make of J.P. but clearly, we were in awe of this perfect child.

Needless to say, I was not like J.P. You might say I was a whole other variety of twelve-year-old. For one thing, I was casual about school assignments. For another, I was obsessed that year. Everything that had filled my life up to that year—piano lessons, reading, games, friends—evaporated in the face of my one all-consuming passion: ice skating. I lived for the three-o-clock school bell that freed me to run all the way home, snatch my newly acquired ice skates and run all the way back, where the play-ground—water-filled each winter—served as the neighborhood ice rink. I skated until dark and walked home glowing and happy.

One day, I ran into a hitch. On that beautiful, clear day, I came upon a disappointing scene following my after-school run to the playground. No skaters and no ice. The playground manager beckoned to me. (By then, we were friends.) He told me that they were working on a problem, but that the ice rink would be back in service within a day or two. Sensing my discontent, he added, "You know, there's a playground with really good skating about a mile from here." He pointed me in that direction and walked off.

The sun was lowering and the air was turning much colder as I walked the long mile. When, finally, the playground was within my line of vision, the weather had turned really cold, with that grey stillness that usually precedes a snow storm. There was a dreamlike quality to the whole scene: no messy gutters, no apartment buildings, no kids out on the street. Just tidy little houses with tidy little front yards. And strangely, not a soul in sight.

I broke into a half-run, swinging my skates, excited over the lovely expanse of ice that surely lay ahead. When I was within mere feet of the playground, suddenly, as if out of thin air, there was J.P.! At first, he was nearly unrecognizable. He stood facing me, perhaps five or six feet in front of me, his arms akimbo, his legs spread apart. The most startling aspect of this scenario was the expression on J.P.'s face. How can I describe it? His features were contorted into a fright mask—open fury dissolving into naked hatred. And me? Confronted with a face the likes of which I had never encountered in all of my twelve years, I stood frozen with fear.

Then, J.P. spoke. No, that's wrong. J.P. shrieked. "Don't you come one step closer, you filthy kike. Take those skates and go home where you belong. We live here so we don't have to put up with you dirty Jews. Do you get me? We don't allow Jews here."

I turned, running. I felt a stinging pain dead-center on my back. That would be J.P. punctuating his message with a handy rock.

The throbbing reminder of J.P.'s rock attack was not the only thing that kept me awake that night. There was just so much to sort out in my mind. The first issue, of course, was the fact of my Jewishness. Up to that time, Jewish was just another of the things that I was. I was brunette, I was female, I was twelve years old. And, I was Jewish. In a home where Papa and Mama always spoke Russian to each other and where the emphasis seemed to focus on "The Russian Intelligentsia" bent on preserving Russian culture and where visitors (as well as Papa's patients) tended to be Russians of varied religions, I probably would have identified myself as Russian. And I guess, if someone had thought to ask, "and, oh yeh, Jewish." After all, went the demographics in my head, wasn't just about everyone Jewish? Well, at least ninety percent, from what I had observed around my neighborhood. That night, I realized my numbers were flawed.

My second issue that sleepless night was hatred. All twelve-year-old girls knew that it was okay to hate for certain twelve-year-old-girl crimes, i.e., telling on you, being two-faced, having gorgeous long blond hair. Hating someone because of the person's religion was a new concept. This was 1934 after all and just short of the time when Hitler made everything clear.

The next morning, I was in my assigned classroom seat when J.P. entered the room. This time, he didn't approach his seat as he did customarily—from the outer, coatroom aisle. He cut over to the middle aisle where I sat. He paused at my desk and waited for me to look up. With eyes half closed, he smiled a broad, close-mouthed smile—catlike—and proceeded to his desk. He sat down and folded his hands and turned his sweet, shining countenance to the door, where Teacher was just entering.

Launching My Brief Career
in Retailing

The year was 1936. It was the summer of my fourteenth year. Mama, an ardent proponent of character-building-through-hard-work (for other people) woke me on a Saturday morning and said, "You need to find a summer job."

In the career consultation that followed, the option of baby-sit-ting was not offered because my parents deemed me too young to be left—even in my own home—alone at night. Go figure.

Hence, heeding Mama's mandate, my exploration of opportu-nities in retailing. The Uptown branch of Goldblatt's department store occupied most of the 4700 block of North Broadway in Chicago. It was close to where we lived and close to Papa's office. On that very Saturday, I walked over to Goldblatt's and was interviewed in their employment office. I was fourteen, looked like a twelve-year-old, and told the nice lady that I was sixteen. She must have known I was lying. She chose me from three equally qualified applicants because, she said, I was "a talker."

So, I was hired on the spot and assigned to Ladies' Sportswear, on the second floor. For those of you who follow fluctuations in the fashion world, you may be interested to learn that bathing suits (the phrase "swim suit" came along much later—around the time toilet paper became toilet tissue) were priced at $1.98 for ordi-nary suits and $2.98 for designer suits. In addition, there was a selection of "tops" (blouses, sweaters) and "bottoms" (shorts, slacks, skirts) all in that same price range. Everything was piled onto open tables and it was my job to wait on customers, assist them in the fitting rooms (long before the advent of air condition-ing) and spend any spare time keeping the piles stacked neatly.

To me, in retrospect, the most interesting aspect of that summer job was the creative manner in which management had swelled the eight-hour day mandated by law, into twelve hours on the job. I was required to begin work at nine a.m. and at noon, allowed two hours for lunch. Then later, I was allowed two hours for dinner, so that although I was eight hours on the job, I was really hooked for twelve hours until my work day ended at nine p.m.

The pay was twenty-five cents per hour.

After finishing at nine p.m. I joined my co-workers in the over-heated store basement in a line that snaked around the room and led to the cashier's cage. About thirty minutes later, when I finally reached the window, I was handed a little sealed brown envelope containing $1.98. The missing sum of two cents was invested into my Social Security account (a brand new innovation—only just established in 1935).

I worked at Goldblatts for three days every week all that summer, and when the summer ended, I had earned a take-home income of $47.52; my Social Security account was off to a running start with a balance of forty-eight cents.

Corned Beef On Lies

The year was 1939. I was seventeen years old. Teddy was twenty-one and Bobby was twenty-three. We were living in an apartment at Agatite and Sheridan. You noticed that? Now, it was Agatite and Sheridan. That was the way with our family. Every year or two, there would be a day when I would come home from school to find Mama waiting at the door with a look that I had learned long ago to recognize. "Glorrhia, Darrhling," she would begin, (Even among her fellow Russians, you'd have ranked her a world-class R-roller.) "pack the books. We're moving." Just like that. No consultation, no advance warning, no anything. Thus would commence my series of treks to the grocery store until I had collected enough boxes for those hundreds of books that we shlepped from apartment to apartment.

When Moving Day arrived, Mama would phone Papa at his office. "Grisha," she would say (I never did discover where that "Grisha" came from; his name was Henry.) "we moved today. I'm calling to tell you the new address."

Today, in retrospect, our apartment-hopping forms a backdrop of markers on my rocky road into the adult world, with specific incidents linked to specific apartments. For Agatite and Sheridan, hands down, it's the Corned Beef Saga—an event wherein the villainy of my brothers found its purest expression.

There was a history to all of this. Bobby and Teddy, from the day that their first male victim rang our doorbell to the day that Herby (brave Herby whose family dynamics had never prepared him really, for my merciless brothers) asked me to marry him, they never let up. Early on, Bobby and Teddy had adopted a routine of assigning quick-reference nicknames to each new entry—usually related to occupation, personality type or off-key physical trait, i.e., Dumbo, The Laundryman, The Goldfish, The Politician. You can understand why, when I expected a date to pick me up, I made sure that I was fully dressed, handbag in hand, near the front door.

One Saturday night, disaster struck. The Laundryman arrived thirty minutes early, while I was in the bath tub. Bobby and Teddy seized the moment. They ushered him into the living room, motioning him to the center seat-cushion of the sofa. They sat down, flanking him on either side, poised to pounce on fresh prey.

Remember: my saga—as is true in most of these stories—must be viewed against a Depression background. This was the very year that my Economics teacher had defined a rich man as someone fortunate enough to be earning $6000.00 peryear. Six thousand! And, to be honest, although money (more precisely the lack of it) was a very big issue with our family—throughout those years, Mama's kitchen was a place where the borsht flowed freely and the solids were plentiful.

But now, here in our living room, sat the Laundryman, whose father owned a commercial laundry—surely, my brothers must have assumed, qualifying him for a place in that heady $6000.00 stratosphere, and most likely ill-prepared to distinguish among the subtle gradations of poorness.

The conversation which follows has been pieced together over the years from gleeful confessions, consistent in their total lack of repentance.

Teddy opened the dialog. "Hey, you're all dressed up. You look really good. Where ya going?"

"Well thanks! It's my birthday and we're going back to my house for my birthday party."

Now, Bobby: "Hey, no kidding! A party. You gonna have food?"

"Well, sure; my mother was fixing up a buffet table when I left just now."

"Wow!" This was Teddy talking. "What's she having?"

"Gee, I dunno. I guess like cold cuts and stuff."

"Cold cuts!"Teddy said, "Ya mean like corned beef?"

"Well, yeh," was The Laundryman's response, "I guess. Why?"

"Why?" shouted Bobby, "You're asking why? I'll tell you why. Because our Relief Basket is late again this month and all we've got left is some powdered eggs and boxes of stale macaroni and cheese. I can't even remember what corned beef tastes like."

Now, finally, Gloria makes her entrance. The two long-legged monsters take off, loping down the bedroom hallway.

So, we left for the party. My driver, The Laundryman, is nearly blinded by tears. My knotted stomach and his grim face during the silent half-hour ride to the party, told me something was amiss. My tentative attempts at damage assessment were met with more silence. I tried for light-hearted and frivolous as befits a Saturday night date. To no avail. Finally, I fell silent, speculating that the story would unfold one way or another before the evening ended.

We walked in on a full house. Twenty-or-so people milling around the dining room table where The Laundryman's mother was playing hostess. The Laundryman inched his way through the crowd and, grasping his mother's elbow, propelled her into the kitchen. When the swinging door closed behind them, I had a sick feeling that this was about me.

Before long, I was caught up in the spirit of the occasion, and except for a few discomfiting moments now and then, when I would catch a glimpse of The Laundryman and his mother exchanging misty-eyed glances in my direction, I gave little thought to the beginning of the evening.

It was a fun party. The ending was one of those endings in which everyone leaves at once. Twenty people in the foyer. A flurry of coats tossed through the crowd. Dialogue about who is riding with whom. But what now? A break in the rhythm. The Laundryman's mother is pushing through to where I stand, grasping my arm and leading me into the kitchen. The door swings shut. She throws her arms around me and bursts into tears. This is a woman I have just met!

I could feel my face flush. I said to her: "Is something wrong?"

Without responding, she opened the refrigerator door and removed a huge tray covered with waxed paper. She thrust it into my arms and said, "Dear, my son and I want your brothers to have this." I was incredulous. "Have what?"

"These are corned beef sandwiches. I wouldn't be able to sleep tonight if I didn't share these with your family."

"No, no!" I protested. "My brothers must have said something to your son, but they are joking all the time. There's been a misunderstanding."

Still misty-eyed, she said, "I won't let you leave without this tray, no matter what you tell me. If your brothers are jokers, tell them a joker sent this to them."

Then, profoundly embarrassed, I walked behind that kind lady, carrying the tray into the foyer.

In The Laundryman's car, homeward bound, there was mostly silence. When we arrived at my stop, The Laundryman removed the tray from the back seat and handed it to me.

"Look," I said, "I can't take this. I don't know what my brothers said to you, but nobody in my family even likes corned beef."

He could not be dissuaded. "I know. I know. Take it anyway."

Not knowing exactly what to do at that point (I was only seventeen, after all.) I took the tray and carried it indoors.

Now it is Sunday morning. I enter the kitchen and find the family seated at breakfast. I scream. "Damn you! Damn you!" (A curse for each brother.) Papa was startled. "Gloria, what's wrong with you?"

I said, "Bobby and Teddy told The Laundryman something I don't know what, but I wanted to die last night." Then, a flood of tears and soothing noises from Papa.

"Gloria dear, calm down. What exactly happened last night?" I poured out the whole miserable story. When I finished—-nothing. Nobody said a word. I looked to Papa—steadfast Papa—ever the strong proponent of Justice for All and I said, "Papa, don't you have anything to say?"

Then, he spoke. Do you know what he said? I am not making this up. He said, "So, where's the corned beef?"

Crossing the Street With Mama

Waldheim Jewish Cemetery was one of a group of adjacent cemeteries in Chicago. It was originally the site of a Pottawottamie Indian burial ground and later, a burial ground for Chicago's early settlers. Then, around 1873, the land became known as Waldheim and was under the aegis of German Masonic Lodges.

In 1969 Waldheim merged with Forest Home Cemetery and the two are now known simply as Forest Home.

To turn-of-the-century Jewish immigrants, and later, to nearly everyone, Waldheim had become synonymous with "cemetery". As in: "If you keep working so hard, you'll end up in the Waldheim."

Now, it is 1940. I am eighteen years old, standing at the corner of Michigan and Randolph with Mama during the evening rush hour. Cars are ripping around the corner. The light says GO.

"Come on, Mama. We have the right-of-way!"

"You'll tell them in the Waldheim that you had the right-of-way."

Mama and My Gentleman Caller

The year was 1941. I was nineteen years old. World War II was getting off the ground and uniformed young men were streaming into Chicago from all over the country to report to Chicago-area military bases. And, not incidentally, to quicken the heart of every hopeful young female Chicagoan. Cousins and aunts and friends living everywhere, were arming their enlisted kin and friends bound for Chicago, with phone numbers of locals who might allay their loneliness. I was the sometimes beneficiary (more often, the victim) of some of that largesse.

This story is about a specific instance that year.

I'm pretty sure it was a Saturday afternoon. I was sitting in the living room reading a book when the phone rang. The caller was a friend of the family inviting me to her home for dinner that night. Inviting only me, which seemed strange indeed. When I arrived, I was greeted by her and her husband (I will refer to them as the D's.) Both were smiling conspiratorially. Mrs. D led me into a bedroom where a chubby uniformed soldier was sound asleep. She said, "This is Sydney (not his real name), my nephew. He is here on a two-week furlough." Now, that's what she <u>said</u>. Her face said, "Be wary—I'm entrusting you with the family jewels." The D's, you see, had no children of their own, and Sydney was their golden boy, I later learned.

Mrs. D rubbed his shoulder gently and awakened him. She cupped her hands around his head and turned his head to face me. Of course, she didn't say "Tada" because people weren't saying that in 1941, but it was like that. As for me, I was taken aback. He was balding and clearly older than my older brothers.

At any rate, we had a few dates, and once or twice we went for daytime walks in the park. (I was between jobs.) Then, one afternoon, about ten days after our meeting, I heard the doorbell. It was Sydney. His face was flushed and it was obvious that he was struggling to maintain his composure. We sat for a while, making light conversation, when suddenly, out of the blue, he dropped to his knees. He said: (You'll just have to take me at my word on this one.) "Gloria, I have fallen in love with you and I want to marry you."

What happened next could have been lifted from a Rosalind Russell comedy.

A key in the front door lock and Mama walking in on this bizarre scenario. Mama: "Why are you on the floor?"

Sydney (red-faced): "I am asking your daughter to marry me."

Mama: "Wouldn't you say this is a little soon?"

Very shortly thereafter—his ardor substantially cooled—Sydney departed. When the door closed behind him, Mama said, "That man is an eediot" (Remember? The Russian accent?)

"Mama," I said, "how can you say that he's an idiot. I'd like you to know that he happens to have a PhD!"

And Mama said? Mama said, "Darrhling, you can send a horse around the world, but it still comes back a horse."

The Fifth "W"—Southern Style

The year was 1944 when I found myself transplanted from my native Chicago to a strange new world: The South. Herb and I had been married only a month or so, living in Charlotte, North Carolina near Herb's post at Morris Field when he received orders to report to Barksdale Field Air Force Base in Shreveport, Louisiana.

During World War II "housing code" was foreign to the Southern vernacular; every conceivable division, addition and revision had been hastily contrived by property owners to accommodate (For patriotism? For profit? Your guess.) the flood of G.I.'s descending on Shreveport.

What we drew out of this mess was one-third of an old wooden house, haphazardly partitioned by a widow named Mrs. LaCuckoo (not her real name but should have been). The other thirds were occupied by Madame herself and a congenial couple from Coffeyville, Kansas. The focal point of our combination bed-room-living room (in another life a screened-in porch) was a gigantic, restaurant-sized refrigerator which could not be fitted into the tiny kitchen. Eventually, that refrigerator became our life-saver during a torrid, non-air-conditioned summer, when Herb, ingenious Herb, simply left the refrigerator door open while a small electric fan whirred in front of it.

The bathroom, which we shared with the other couple, had a single window which opened up onto our "apartment", which made sense when the room had been a porch. In this new configuration, party guests and housemates inclined to open the window, were greeted by an unwelcome audience.

Ruby, our house-sharing army bride, lost no time landing a job operating the switchboard in the Shreveport Journal building. As for me, my soldier husband was gone for long hours at a stretch and I was more or less left to my own devices.

One mid-morning, the postman delivered a wedding gift. I unwrapped it on the bedroom floor and then, while I was in the kitchen looking for a trash bag, I heard a rustling of the tissue wrappings. I went back to investigate. I froze as I stood eyeball-to-eyeball with a dog-size rat, which most likely had emerged from the hole in the floor where the former refrigerator had been. I screamed. I stamped my foot. The rat not only held its ground, it never once turned its head away from me. I flew out of the apartment into Mrs. LaCuckoo's living room. I found her seated, stirring her usual morning libation of tea laced with a touch of boozy pick-me-up.

"There's a rat in there! A really big rat! Do something!"

She placed the teaspoon on the edge of the saucer. She shook her head in disgust. She folded her arms. "The janitor comes Tuesday. I'll have him take care of it."

"<u>Tuesday</u>? This is Friday! What are you talking about? I can't go back in there with that thing in my apartment!"

Mrs. LaCuckoo rose from her chair. Slowly. With all of the wartime-landlady contempt that she could muster, she spat out: "Child, you must be from the <u>North</u>." And with that, she did, literally, push me out of her door.

I had mentioned to Ruby that I might try to find a job and she had said that after Herb and I were settled, I might want to apply for a part-time clerical opening at the Journal. Now, since returning to the apartment was out of the question, I decided to give it a shot. I began to walk in the direction of downtown Shreveport when I found myself at the Journal building. It was just about noon.

Inside, I heard nothing and I saw nobody. I wandered around the building and eventually walked through a door labeled "City Room". There, I spotted a lone man seated inside of a glass-walled enclosure. When he noticed me, he said, "Young lady, are you looking for somebody?"

I said, "I wanted to apply for a job here, but it looks like I picked the wrong time."

"No," he assured me, "it's just that everyone is out to lunch. I'm Doug Attaway, the publisher. Are you a reporter?"

"Uh, yes—yes, I'm a reporter. Are there openings for reporters?"

He leaned back in his chair. "Missy, tell me where you're from. Tell me where you're living here in Shreveport. Tell me a little about yourself."

We talked briefly and then he explained, "We're in a fix here. We've taken a big loss of reporters and feature writers to the military draft. We have a list to draw from but that takes time. Of course, we can't pay you what your big-city paper was likely paying you."

I assured him that I knew how those things went. This is what he said next: (Actually, this is how it sounded to me.) "We had a phone call this morning from a man who said he caught himself a 200 pound turtle down by Bikham by you. Here's the man's phone number. Now, you go call him and then you go write it up, and then, Little Missy, you turn it in to Bill Williams. He's my city editor. When you finish your supper tonight (The Journal was an evening paper.) go out and buy a Shreveport Journal. If you're hired, you'll find your story and byline on the front page. If you don't see it, don't come to work."

I walked out of his office, mulling over what I had just heard. First of all, the "where" W of those five W's learned in Journalism 101 had certainly pertained to something more specific than "by you". Secondly, the phrase "by you", occasionally heard in Chicago as in "How's by you?" or "Did they come visit by you?" was used primarily by ethnic groups with limited command of the English language. Now, what was I to make of a newspaper publisher talking like that?

At any rate, I found some copy paper on a nearby desk and sat down to phone the turtle hunter. I took copious notes as he rendered a play-by-play account of his exploit. Then, I asked, "Where, exactly, did you catch the turtle?"

He responded, "Down by Bikham by you." Now, I was really at a loss. Clearly, Mr. Attaway had already talked with him and told him where I lived. Strange! But, still, where <u>was</u> this Bikham by me? I hung up and, seeing that there was no one around to question, I simply decided to work around the problem and cite the location as Bikham. Period. I typed my story and deposited it on the desk bearing Mr. Williams' name plate. I left the building.

I wandered the streets until it was time for Herb's return from the base. He entered the apartment first and was kind enough to spare me the details of his rat-expunging, assuring me that now I would be comfortable waiting until Tuesday for the janitor.

The weather was stifling that evening and we opted for the relief of the air-conditioned base movie theater. As we waited in line out on the field, I filled Herb in on the details of my interview. He left the line to purchase a copy of the Journal. There it was on Page One: my byline story. The headline: "Local Man Captures 200-Pound Turtle at Bikham Bayou."

If you live in Chicago, pay attention here:

A bayou is a marshy, sluggish body of water, tributary to a lake or river. It is a Louisiana French adaptation of the Choctaw Indian "bayuk".

What Did McCarthy Want With A Nice Jewish Girl Like Me?

The year was 1950. Herb and I had moved from Chicago to Washington, D.C. towards the end of 1948, so that he could apply his newly acquired Labor Economics degree in the service of the welfare fund newly initiated by the United Mine Workers of America. The dearth of postwar housing posed a problem, but finally, we landed a passable apartment in Mt. Ranier, Maryland.

Once we were settled in, I decided to seek a job. I hoped that my short stint at <u>The Shreveport Journal</u> plus a variety of earlier writing, editing and advertising jobs, would qualify me for a shot at something with the U.S. Government's <u>Voice of America</u> program.

I got wind of a writing position that seemed tailor-made for my skills and interests. I visited the agency and spoke with an amiable interviewer who sent me home with the appropriate employment form, which I hastily filled in and submitted. The agency's rapid response surprised and delighted me. I was hired, they informed me, and I was instructed where and when to report for work.

Then, out of the blue, a few days later, I received a follow-up "not-so-fast-honey" letter informing me that I had a choice of appearing at a hearing (time and place indicated therein) or simply not accepting the job. My employment could not go forward, they indicated, because of security concerns. I was young then, and had, up to that time, been more-or-less apolitical and could not for the life of me imagine anything other than a case of mistaken identity.

The root cause of all of this, of course, was the flaming McCarthyism rampant in the U.S. from the late forties into the early fifties. Celebrities from every walk of life were fingered indiscriminately for mostly unfounded Communist leanings. The atmosphere was one of inquisition and sensationalist investigatory methods. Careers were ruined or put on hold.

But moi? Why, I asked myself, why would those important people bothering those important people bother with <u>me</u>?

I thought it over for a while and decided that since Herb was launched on his career track and likely to be affected by any shadow cast on me, it would be best to go ahead and appear at the hearing. Just for the record, I had only the vaguest idea of what a hearing <u>was</u>; hence, I arrived on the specified date without a clue.

I was ushered into a room where a long conference table was already ringed by several somber-looking men and one kindly-looking older woman. Nobody was smiling. Almost immediately, the questioning began. What follows are the transgressions upon which (I ultimately learned) my "case" was based.

My first transgression centered around my second high school-age job in retailing. A friend had tipped me off to a "hosiery girl" opening at a downtown shoe store. In those days, hosiery girls were positioned alongside cashiers to push stocking sales when shoe purchases were consummated. It was a coveted job for teenagers. I had been warned that I might need a fuller job resume than my experience with Goldblatts selling ladies sportswear. I prevailed upon our neighborhood pharmacist. He assured me that if anyone phoned him, he would say that I had indeed worked for him. In fact, I had not, but in those days, it was ya-gotta-do-what-ya-gotta-do to find any kind of job. The hearing revealed that this kindly gentleman had (or so they claimed) a Communist affiliation.

I guess you might say that the lie was a Depression-inspired lie. The second lie that brought me to the hearing, was a postwar-inspired lie.

When Herb was discharged from military service, there had been virtually no new construction anywhere in Chicago during the war years; the housing shortage was critical. Immediately after his arrival in Chicago, we moved into the back bedroom of his parents' apartment and began our search for a place to live. It seemed hopeless. Then, after weeks of searching, Herb was attending to some business in downtown Chicago and, realizing he had a free hour, dropped in on an old Air Force buddy whose office was in the vicinity.

They chatted and Herb mentioned how eager he was to get settled if only we could find a place to live. As Herb was leaving the office, he was stopped by the man's secretary. She said, "Forgive me, Sir, but I could not help but overhear your conversation and I may be able to help you. I have a small apartment on the south side and I am moving to California soon. There is always a long waiting list for our apartments, but preference is given to relatives of tenants. I am willing to tell management that you are related to me if you are willing to purchase certain of my effects, such as stemware and such." (That was the postwar-housing euphemism for "I expect you to pay me a bribe for getting you this apartment.")

Herb agreed with enthusiasm. Our back bedroom overlooking the garbage pails was by now pretty gamey. But how could we have known then (as I was learning now, years later) that this bogus "relative" whom we had paid so handsomely for the apartment, was actually on her way to California to take a high position (at least that's what they told me at the hearing) with the Communist party?

Those were the two primary accusations. There were some other peripheral ones almost too outlandish to mention, i.e., did my physician father (he had died nine years earlier.) ever write prescriptions specifying that they were to be filled by a Communist pharmacist?

Sounds pretty bizarre today, doesn't it?

Well, here is what happened next. As this pugnacious interrogation became increasingly irrational, finally, a voice of sanity drowned out the madness . It was that lone woman—Mrs. Henry

Grattan Doyle. She spoke up for the first time and defended me vociferously, pointing out to my questioners the absurdity of the entire scenario. And the hearing ended then and there.

Soon after that, I received a letter from the Federal Government informing me that I was cleared of all charges and that I was free to pursue a career in government. By then, I had landed an interesting job with an ad agency, having been forewarned by more seasoned Washingtonians that "once you've had a hearing, no agency will touch you." And that's the way it was when McCarthy was spooking all of this country with his delusions.

Since then, I have learned a little about Mrs. Henry Grattan Doyle. I learned that she had been Dean of the Columbia College of George Washington University, and that in 1955 she won the John Benjamin Nichols Award, presented yearly to "a lay person, organization, or both, in recognition of outstanding contributions toward improving the health of the community."

My Brother Teddy
The Comeback Kid

The year was 1957. Lynn was a year old and Laurie was four. Herb was away at a conference in Arizona when I received a phone call from Brother Teddy.

"I'm here in Miami Beach with Helene and the kids at a place called the Carousel Motel. The unit next to ours is vacant, so how about bringing the kids down for a week?"

How about bringing the kids down for a week? In a heartbeat! I tossed aside the toilet brush still resting in my free hand and threw a hit-or-miss Miami Beach wardrobe into the first piece of luggage that fell from the closet shelf. We arrived in Miami Beach the very next day.

The next morning we were poolside by eight o'clock. No one else was in sight. Helene shepherded all five children into the empty pool: Laurie and Lynn plus their Frances, age four, Iris, age three and Greg, age one. Teddy settled into a lounge chair and I settled in to his right. Then, a lone man appeared. Picture it: a solid row of unoccupied lounge chairs ringing the entire pool, close enough to touch. But that man seated himself on the chair next to Teddy.

Our newcomer arranged himself with some deliberation: first, he pulled his Shlitz Beer cap lower onto his forehead. Then, he performed a trim-cut-spit ritual to get his cigar burning. Finally, he folded his hands over his ample belly and surveyed the scene.

He turned to face Teddy. He removed his sunglasses. He said, "Cripes, looka that broad in the pool!" Teddy poked my ribs with his elbow. "What about her?"

"Well, for starters, she's built like a brick shit-house."

Teddy and I stared straight ahead, not replying.

The man, no doubt suspecting that his language had been offensive, took another track: "I'll say one thing for her, though. She's a heluva good mother."

And Teddy said? Teddy leaned to face the man even closer, and said, "She damn well better be. Those are my kids."

The Queen (Actually, Her Emissary)
Was in the Counting House
Counting Out the Likes of Me

It was in the '60's when Herb, in the course of his work, was associated for a time with the labor attache of the British embassy in Washington, D.C. that we were placed on the guest list for the queen's birthday party.

You need to understand about the queen's birthday party. Number One, she doesn't really show up. Number Two, it isn't held on her actual birthday. Number Three, it is held at British embassies all over the world on the same non-birthday day each year.

Well, you know we went. Wouldn't anyone? And it was fascinating. The flurry around the arriving limousines, the women in their gossamer dresses and marvelous oversize hats; some even wore little white gloves. And hundreds of guests milling around the embassy's expansive manicured lawn, pausing every now and then for refills at the various stations dispensing strawberries and Devonshire cream—the traditional Queen's Birthday refreshment.

The invitation did not extend to entry into the embassy itself, but an open door leading into the foyer revealed a large, imposing portrait of Queen Elizabeth II displayed at the stair landing.

I viewed the whole experience as a once-in-a-lifetime colorful deposit into my memory bank, so you can imagine what a delight it was to receive an invitation for the next year's party. And the year after that—-long after Herb's affiliation with his British contact had ended. Herb—-wise in the ways of Washington—-explained patiently that "Once you get onto these embassy guest lists, you need to do something really gauche to get off." I asked, "Like what?" He said, "Oh, I don't know—maybe pee on the embassy grounds."

Happily, I remained continent and the invitations kept coming. Then, one year there was no invitation. As I was puzzling over its absence, I happened to turn to a story in the Style section of The Washington Post. It was an interview with the wife of the newly appointed British ambassador to Washington. I am paraphrasing here.

"As the wife of the newly appointed British ambassador, what do you consider your first priority?"

"My first priority has been to rid our guest lists of dead wood."
Another case closed.

Ben, They Made The Pants All Wrong

The year was 1967. Lynn was eleven years old—the half-woman, half-child time when girls are down the middle between a fading interest in Barbie dolls and a nascent interest in nylon panty hose. Lynn's campaign for her first pair of panty hose had been going on for about six months.

Please indulge me; before I continue with this saga, you need to know about Gershman's.

Beginning when Lynn and Lauren were around middle-school age and well into their late teens, we owned a modest condo apartment in Dewey Beach, Delaware—a resort town adjacent to Rehoboth Beach, Delaware. In Rehoboth Beach proper, on Rehoboth Avenue, on the ocean block, there was Gershman's.

Gershman's was a hunters-and-gatherers store where one dug into piles of sportswear on rows of tables, searching for that elusive designer label mixed in with Ben Gershman's latest job-lot of manufacturers' jumbled residue. For me and for my beach friends, on rainy days at the beach, Gershman's was the hottest show in town. So it happened that on one rainy Saturday morning, I was greeted by Ben's wife, Sylvia, who was eager to share the news of their latest coup. They had made a purchase of a huge shipment of panty hose and "today only" were selling them at three pairs for one dollar. At that price, I decided I could indulge Lynn.

At the cash register, I asked Ben if the hose were irregular. He said, "Well yes, but nothing that would affect the wear." I purchased three pairs in Lynn's size.

Now, it is Monday morning and Lynn's friends, Robin and Jodie, are waiting in our foyer while Lynn dresses for school. I run upstairs to hurry her along and find her furiously tugging and pulling at the panty hose—clearly exasperated.

I said, "Lynn, I cannot believe this; a big girl like you can't do something as simple as putting on a pair of stockings!" She began to cry. I said, "Look, lie back on the bed and I'll help you."

I took the panty hose and pushed and pulled until I managed to work the top up to her waistline. And then? And then, I discovered that the feet pointed backwards!

The following weekend, at the beach again, I showed the panty hose to Ben Gershman. He examined them. He said, "Well, like I told you, there's nothing here that would affect the wear."

(Alas, factory outlet malls are now clustered along the Eastern Shore and Gershman's has gone by the wayside.)

Emergency Surgery
On A Diamond Ring

I can't say that diamonds were ever my best friends. When Herb and I were married during World War II, even the thought of a diamond ring would have been ludicrous, considering the state of our finances. For the twenty-five years that followed, I was barely aware of the gold band on my ring finger and certainly had no interest in upgrading.

Then in 1969 as our twenty-fifth wedding anniversary approached, Herb embarked on a secret mission that culminated in my acquisition of a wedding ring fashioned of tiny diamond baguettes encased in platinum. Herb's mother's cousin, a diamond dealer based in South Africa, was visiting New York, and Herb, on the pretense of a business trip, arranged to meet with him so that they could hand-select each little baguette. Of course, I learned of all this long after the fact. At any rate, on March 11, 1969 on the morning of our twenty-fifth wedding anniversary, Herb presented the ring to a tearful recipient. I slipped it on.

Early the very next morning, my friend Nadine, who had an eye for such things, stopped by for coffee. She deemed it a classic beauty and asked if she could view it more closely. I tried to slip it off. It wouldn't budge. I pulled. I twisted. I pushed it up. I pushed it down. Nothing. So, what did I do? I panicked.

Over the period of that entire week, I phoned everyone I could think of, seeking advice. Just for the record, this is a partial list of the solutions offered in that one week:

Apply an ice pack and then oil your finger.
Coat your finger with petroleum jelly.
Soak your finger in cold, soapy water.
Soak your finger in Windex.
Soak your entire hand in ice water.
Relax your finger and wait.
Take a sizable length of string or dental floss, wrap it several times around your knuckle and slip the end of the string through the ring and pull gently so that the string will unwind and the ring will come off. (This one, I found a little difficult to envision much less implement.)
Ask a jeweler to cut it off.

Above all, do not go to the emergency room because those people will damage your ring.

Trust me when I tell you that I labored long and hard over those home remedies. The result? More swelling—more pain. Finally, when my finger began to bleed at the site of the ring, it was clear that it was time for professional intervention. I carried my problem to a jeweler in the Wheaton Plaza shopping mall. He looked at the swollen, bloody mess and explained that once there was bleeding, he was forbidden by law from cutting off the ring.

I went home to wait for Herb, all the while adding to the problem by continuing to work at the ring.

At about ten o'clock that night, we did the only thing left to do. We drove to the emergency room of the Holy Cross Hospital in Silver Spring, Maryland.

When the admitting clerk saw the ring and heard my problem, she ushered me inside instantly. I was assigned to a bed where I lay for some time, waiting for attention. The drawn curtain on my right, separated me from what sounded like an elderly man clearly in distress.

Throughout the emergency room, word spread quickly about my dilemma, and a gaggle of female staffers crowded around my bed to witness the resolution of my problem. When the hospital's official ring-cutter showed up, carrying his box of knives, excitement mounted. How was he going to relieve this situation without destroying my diamonds? I asked him how much experience he'd had in his unique specialty and he admitted that I was his first <u>live</u> victim; his actual job description had more to do with relieving corpses of their worldly goods.

While Holy Cross's official ring cutter was going through his paces, carefully and slowly (but fruitlessly) trying one knife at a time, his female audience was breathless.

Not so the patient behind the curtain. After the ring-cutter had been fiddling around with his knives for perhaps fifteen minutes, the curtain on my right was flung open to reveal an elderly man struggling out of his bed, visibly disgusted with what he had been hearing. He said, "I am a retired jeweler. Get out of my way!"

He examined the box of knives. One by one, he tossed each one aside, each time saying, "This is no good! This is no good!" Then, he picked up the very last knife in the box, and only then he said, "This is good!"

Whereupon-despite his visible pain-he cut the ring open without destroying one single baguette!

Seer With Clouded Vision

The year was 1974. Lynn was eighteen and Laurie was twenty-one. We moved that year. Although the move was a mere fifteen minutes removed from the suburban home of her childhood, this grander house in the city was too giant a leap for Lynn. She longed for the old neighborhood. She missed the proximity of her friends. She ached for the house that held her childhood memories. She was miserable. Vociferously miserable. She was way past getting on everyone's nerves.

Now, here we are on a Sunday morning, settling into the new house. Lynn has taken her case to the street. Herb and Laurie and I realized as much when we responded to a deafening, subhuman wail emanating from the front of the house. We—all three—rushed outdoors to find Lynn on the front stoop, rocking back and forth, bellowing at an intensity that would have filled her drama teacher with pride. This was too much. Sympathy was out the window.

We half-dragged, half-coaxed Lynn into the privacy of the living room for the type of confrontation that rarely occurred in our family—a genuine, old-fashioned shouting match.

Just as the decibel level was rocketing through the roof, the phone rang. I ran to the kitchen to catch the call. This is what I heard: "Mrs. Liebenson, you don't know me, but I have taken the liberty of phoning you because our husbands are friends. My name is Jeane Dixon. I've heard about those interesting new houses they've built over there and I was wondering whether today would be convenient for me to pop over." (We had purchased the first of eighty houses in that picturesque enclave.)

Surely you've heard of Jeane Dixon. For decade after decade until her death in 1997 at age seventy-nine, she was the horse's mouth for every conceivable type of prognostication. Her skills were sought after all over the world. Her predictions of campaign outcomes were published far and wide. Her name was synonymous with astrology.

The famous Jeane Dixon was asking to come to our house! Of course, I urged her to come right over. She estimated it would take about twenty minutes to get there.

Back in the living room, the battle was still raging. When I reported that the legendary Jeane Dixon was arriving in mere minutes, Herb presented Lynn with a series of restrictions on her freedom that extended well into the year 2000 if she so much as opened her mouth to breathe.

When our distinguished guest arrived, I escorted her into the living room and introduced her (momentary truce prevailing) to my family, and then escorted her through the house. When we reached the dining room, which had a wrought-iron "fence" overlooking the sunken living room, that sweet, bird-like lady grasped the rail of the fence with her white-gloved hands. She raised her head and faced the ceiling. She closed her eyes. She exhaled.

And then? And then, she said, "I sense a strange and beautiful peace within these walls. I feel happiness flowing through my veins. What fortunate people you are to be so content!"

She said Goodbye and she left.

My Couturier Dry Cleaner

The year was 1975. Back then, there still were a few old-fashioned dry-cleaning establishments, owner-operated by dedicated professionals who knew their customers by name. Our neighborhood dry cleaner, Mr. L. was one of them. He favored Herb and me particularly, I believe, because his name was almost the same as ours.

Mr. L. loved fine fabrics. On more than one occasion, when business was slow, he would spread out our incoming garments and comment about the content, quality, beauty or, sometimes, inferiority, of the fabric.

Nineteen Seventy-Five, it so happens, was the year I achieved a significant weight loss (which I sustained for perhaps two weeks). I rushed up to the attic immediately, to collect all of the lovely old size ten clothes stored there until the glorious day when I could use them again. As Herb and I were stuffing the clothes into a laundry bag, Herb said, "Just look at these beautiful fabrics. Just look at the workmanship. Mr. L. hasn't seen anything like these dresses in a long time."

I tossed the bag into my car and when I arrived at the store, Mr. L. was alone at the counter. I overturned the bag. My clothing covered the entire counter. I was watching Mr. L. carefully. I said, "Mr. L. so what do you think of all this?"

He lifted one piece and studied it. Then another, and then a third. Finally, he shook his head and said, "I'll tell you what I think. I think you eat like my wife."

Bad Dog And Englishman

We're still in 1975. A gorgeous spring morning and I was out for my walk with the late Soko, our beloved Shitzu. My friend, the late Helen Nash, beckoned me from her tiny kitchen balcony. "Come on up for some coffee," she shouted. "Can't," I answered, "I have Soko." "That's okay," she said, "he can't do any harm. Come on."

I went upstairs into her kitchen and started to tie Soko's leash to a chair. Helen took the leash from me. "Oh, let him wander," she said, "he'll be okay."

So, Soko wandered, inspecting every corner of Helen's big house while we gossiped and drank coffee. After an hour or so, I recalled that Helen was expecting visitors from England that day, so I collected Soko and left.

That evening, Helen phoned me. She reported that her visitors had been enchanted with her beautiful home and requested a house tour. Helen obliged, and when they were in the downstairs family room, the British gentleman said to Helen, "This is all very lovely indeed—and I assume you have an animal?" The question puzzled Helen. She assured him that there were no pets in her house.

After the visitors left, Helen returned to the family room to tend to the lights. In the corner of the room, there was a neatly stacked pile of excrement.

Letter From Singapore

Trade Association: An association of merchants or business firms for the unified promotion of their common interests. (New World Dictionary, Second College Edition)

Washington, D.C. is the mother lode of trade associations. Proximity to the powers-that-be on Capitol Hill, makes Washington a logical venue for the 700-or-so business and professional trade associations headquartered there. There are trade associations elsewhere, but Washington seems to be where it's at.

Herbert Liebenson, my late husband, was an executive with the National Small Businessmen's Association for many years, where he lobbied for legislation that would protect and advance the interests of small business. (Small business, I learned from Herb, is a far more inclusive group than one might assume. For instance, while the corner grocery store is a small business, so is a bigger business that is small for its industry. Hence a furniture manufacturer with a hundred employees might fall into that category.)

In 1983, during the time that Herb was serving as President, he received the following letter from a retired commodore residing in Singapore. I am not sure but I think that letter was responsible for the association's name change from the National Small Businessmen's Association to the National Small Business Association. What do you think?

royal tanjung pinang yacht club

PATRON: H.R.H. PRINCE LEONARD OF HUTT

Headquarters: 3010 International Plaza
10 Anson Rd
Singapore 0207
Tel 2230016
TLX. RS 26971

Branch Office: Lorong Merdeka IV 513D
Tanjung Pinang
Indonesia
Tel: 21975

INTERNATIONAL MAILING ADDRESS

Maxwell Rd. Post Office
BOX 10 2456
Singapore 9044

The President

National Small Businessmans Association

1604 K St, NW,

Washington, DC 20006

U.S.A.

01AUGUST83'

Dear Sir,

One of the Royal Tanjung Pinang Yacht Club's founding fathers, Mr. H. Gutow, has withdrawn from all social contacts with the club recently. Mr. Gutow is of very short statue, being only 4 ft. 8inches tall; and; apparently his withdrawl followed some slight offered Gutow, and intended as a joke. I am a long standing friend of Mr Gutow and know that he is very sensitive about his height but it is a very difficult issue to raise without seeming to make fun of the man.

I wondered if your organization might have some kind of pamphlets or literature that might make approaches to Mr Gutow easier; everything I have done seems in vain.

I would greatly appreciate hearing from you.

Yours Sincerely,

Vincent Keane

Vincent Keane   RN (Ret.)

72

Vivian

The year was 1986. Another seven-year mark and the Robins were right on target. Edith and Mort Robins, our long-time interior design clients, refurbished their Silver Spring, Maryland home at precise seven-year intervals beginning not too long after Faye Rosen Wolf and I had established our interior design partnership. The 1986 project was the second of many.

To know that household, you need first of all, to know about Vivian—the linchpin that kept the wheels spinning throughout the better part of the Robins' marriage. Vivian—housed in a basement suite—suffered silently (most of the time) and worked diligently through the trials and tribulations of housekeeping, raising the three Robins daughters and tending to Mort's demanding resident mother.

Mort's mother's presence was complicated by a heart condition that precluded a lot of stair climbing. In fact, her cardiologist had ordered her to remain in her upstairs quarters and to descend only once a week for Sunday dinner.

While Edith and Mort labored at their government careers, Vivian was autonomous. She ran the family; she ran the house.

What interested me most about Vivian was her dual personality. In the presence of the Robins family, she was elegant and ladylike, going so far as to assume Edith's Boston speech pattern, so that their voices were indistinguishable on the phone. On the other hand, when I was alone with Vivian, she viewed me as a fellow employee and her language was foul and ungrammatical.

On a particular day during that 1986 project, I found myself lacking a dimension needed for a carpet estimate. Vivian was home alone when I arrived. I was belly-down on the floor, pushing a tape measure under the sofa, when the doorbell rang.

Vivian opened the door to a television repairman. While he was arranging his gear, he said to Vivian, "I can't understand how anything could have gone wrong. I just installed this thing two weeks ago."

Vivian said, "They's a mean, wicked old lady upstairs. She stay in the bed six days a week. On the seventh day, she come downstairs and fuck up my whole house."

Random Thoughts About My Aging Children and Their Elderly Mother

I am writing this in 2004 but these notions began to take shape back in 1999 when I received a phone call from my friend Deevee. She was living in Florida then, but a long time ago, when we were both young, we were chums in our native Chicago. Our ways parted around the time that her curly-headed imp of a daughter named Teddi was learning to crawl.

Deevee and I talked for a long time. We recalled girlhood memories and shared a few laughs. And then I asked, "Tell me, where is little Teddi?" She said, "Little Teddi is in menopause."

Lately, Deevee had been fighting serious medical problems and she dwelt at length on Teddi's present role in her life. "Child hardly fits." she explained, " She's my friend and my case manager and my caretaker."

That was the kind of talk I could really relate to. Barely six months earlier, with Herb hospitalized and with our pending move from our big old house into an apartment, our daughter Lynn took over like a pro. This miracle daughter of ours—football mom, mother of two who works full time and manages Swedish pancake Sunday breakfasts for forty-odd neighborhood kids—somehow managed to engineer every detail of the move, out and in.

Once the move was accomplished, our daughter Lauren, a Seattle-based eldercare executive, arrived in Washington, D.C. to lend her experience and good sense to the cause of her father's recuperation.

Now, some three years after their father's death, both daughters are empathic and caring. They are there for me.

The conversation with my Florida friend, plus that recent experience with our daughters, set me to thinking that although the "sandwich generation" guidebooks flood the market these days, there's a dearth of guidelines for my generation—newly face-to-face with "children" eligible for AARP membership. I look at these aging children and I think to myself, who among us could have predicted the craziness of the '60's metamorphosing into my friend's sons, now balding, somber men and yes, those menopausal women coming forward to direct our third act.

Actually, aging children/aging parents is somewhat of a new phenomenon. A baby born in 1900 had a life expectancy of 47.3 years. If you were a sixty-five-year-old male in 1996 you have 15.7 additional years. For women: even better—18.9 more years.

If only Dr. Spock had anticipated this whole new population and written a final chapter to coach us through the de-parenting of these worthy offspring. Lacking that final chapter, I guess we just have to muddle along defining our interaction with them. What I discovered was that once loosened from the clutch of parenting, our hands are free to embrace these new-found friends: the adults who evolved out of that parenting.

I discovered that you really have to clean the slate. That means letting go of the past and creating a new present. Our offspring are powerless to carry this off; it has to be us. We're the ones who need to burn that burdensome baggage of Terrible Twos and Turbulent Teens.

I remember reading in a child psychology textbook that a study conducted by an individual named Hartley observed that very young children, when informed that the postman is also a daddy, will see him "limited to the single role in which he is momentarily observed...." A postman is a postman. And, most of the time, a parent is a parent—perhaps stemming from parents' reluctance to give up parenting long after parenting is appropriate. Some people I know have carried this to extremes—with dependence-inducing financial subsidies, enabling of substance abuse and illegality, or simply in their condescending demeanor.

My dear friend Zelda Porte, a psychotherapist who specializes in family relationships, notes that "It is particularly hard, I believe, for children of any age to see a parent in any other role than that of parent."

Some years ago, during a visit to New York City, Herb and I ran into an 85-year-old gentleman we had known some years earlier. He was pleased to see us, but apologized for rushing on because he was late for the office. We expressed surprise, having heard that he had long ago turned over the management of his business to his son.

"Well," he explained, "I still feel that I have to be there at least three days a week. I just don't feel that he's sufficiently seasoned." His son was 63 years old.

What we parents <u>should</u> seek from these grownup "kids" of ours is warm and loving friendship—ideally, all of us positioned eyeball-to-eyeball. We all know it ain't gonna happen while we're treating middle-aged adults like ten-year-olds.

For me, this realization didn't come overnight, but once I had it figured out, I realized that it was necessary to let go of the past and put a new imprint on a shining tabula rasa—that fresh, clean slate. In short, I think that our adult children deserve the same respect we accord to cherished friends—because then, hopefully, they too will be our cherished friends.

An Unexpected Twist
Sours My First Tryst

If anything in the preceding pages has led you to believe that I ever was worldly in affairs of the heart, let me disabuse you of that notion. For the fifty-seven years of my marriage, I was the model of monogamy. Then, after Herb's death in 2001 I busied myself with college classes, ballet, theater, a piano gifted to me by my friends, the Cappellos, when they moved away to Florida. And, of course, still a little bit of interior design, as well as writing. I missed Herby. A lot. Still, I felt a certain contentment in my well-organized life.

Then, along came Borden.

Borden came into my life (as I came into my 80's) courtesy of a wonderful friend and neighbor named Anne Zim. I met her early-on in our water aerobics class and almost from the start, she talked at length about an Uncle Borden living in Connecticut. "You have so much in common," she said, "and the next time he's in D.C. you really must get together."

Borden, a retired movie producer and educator, sure enough eventually appeared in person—to further research a book in-work about a World War II hero. He was in town for five days. We dined together five nights. The rest is history.

I am telling you this as a prologue to the story of my first tryst. A tryst may not seem momentous to you, but it was major to a life-time traditionalist like me.

My scenario takes shape from an invitation to Nancy Kahan—another niece of Borden's—from her brother, offering his home in Spring Lake, New Jersey for her use while he and his wife visited

Ireland. It is unclear to me whether there was an implied extension of that invitation, to include Borden and me; Nancy with her Main Squeeze and Susan, Nancy's friend. Were we <u>really</u> invited? I prefer not to linger there.

I arrived by train. Susan drove down from New York. Borden and Nancy drove together and Borden—out of what I hope was happy anticipation—managed to forget his luggage. Soon after we settled in, Borden and Nancy and I climbed into Borden's car to shop for replacement clothes for Borden. Nancy, the driver, backed into a neighbor's car. Although the damage was minimal, the accident somehow sets the scene for our weekend from hell.

Upon our arrival, we saw, near the kitchen phone, a gracious note from the owners, addressed to Nancy—urging her to enjoy their lovely home, but cautioning her to exert extra care with the kitchen floor. It had been laid just recently with "costly wood" and it needed special care. "If you do happen to spill anything," the note said, "please wipe it up instantly." The floor was the only part of the house specified in their welcoming note.

Now, with the car-damaged neighbor mollified and Borden's hit-or-miss new vacation wardrobe in place, our party of five sat down to a cozy alfresco dinner. Someone in the group discovered a video in the parlor—"Little Women"—and, in what must have been a moment of group nostalgia, we all sat back for a movie night.

At about ten or so, after the movie ended and people were beginning to scatter, I told Borden that I disliked waking up to dirty dishes. "Borden," I said, "let's you and I go in there and between us, we can polish it up in no time."

Standing side-by-side at the kitchen sink in that enormous kitchen, we began to organize the supper debris, with Borden pushing the food waste into the disposer. When he turned it on, we heard the grinding sound of metal-on-metal and he quickly pushed the button that turned it off. I reached over to investigate the offending sound and Borden brushed my arm aside and thrust his hand in instead.

And, that was the prelude to the nightmare that ensued.

Borden turned to me. He said, "I cannot remove my hand from this thing."

Borden has a great sense of humor; I said, "Come on, Borden, that ain't funny." Borden's face turned visibly whiter. "I am dead serious. My hand is stuck in this disposer."

Borden pinched his fingers together. Borden twisted his hand. Borden pumped his hand up and down. Nothing changed. Nothing except more pain and bleeding with each attempt to free his hand. I summoned the others. We all agreed that our prospects for a solution were dimmed mightily by the limited local facilities in this charming but very small town. I suggested that we begin with a phone call to 911.

Did I mention that there was a heavy rainstorm that night? The last thing on the minds of that contingent of four booted firemen who responded, was the preservation of our host's kitchen floor. The firemen were only the beginning; they, as one could have predicted, didn't have a clue re solving our problem. At that point, Borden had been standing in an unnatural bent-over position and he was growing faint.

Me? I was one hundred percent in character: rolled up in a ball in the corner of the living room sofa.

The fireman in charge summoned the police. Minutes later, two personable young policemen appeared—one of whom was scheduled to leave for Ireland the next morning along with his bride-to-be. The policemen scratched their heads. Said <u>they</u> didn't have a clue. I uncurled from my fetal ball and overturned a tall umbrella stand so that Borden could—though his hand was in the disposer—sit on something. The Ireland-bound policeman phoned his retired plumber uncle, who appeared on the scene in mere minutes. By then it was midnight, hence the official start of Borden's birthday. Nobody sang.

The elderly ex-plumber carried us to the edge of terror, i.e., this was a type of disposer—no longer manufactured—comparable to the road surfacing that is designed to destroy your tires if you back up. He then proceeded to loosen some of the underparts of the disposer, resulting in (with less underneath to support his hand) Borden's vociferous cries of added pain and bleeding.

As you can see, our host's kitchen was filling up: four firemen, two policemen and one plumber. Outside, in this quiet little enclave (past midnight): one fire truck, one police car, one pickup truck. And the rain—now torrential. And on this lovely new kitchen floor: rain-soaked muddy boots plus assorted metal parts from the undersink cabinet

Time for "What next?" Of course—The Rescue Squad! At this point, a mysterious middle-aged man (a neighbor?) enters and positions himself in a far corner of the kitchen, where he remains until the bitter end, never uttering a word.

The entire Spring Lake Volunteer Rescue Squad responded— again, instantaneously, and seemed to, literally, pour into the kitchen. Count them: there are now nineteen people (including Borden) in this formerly pristine kitchen.

The Rescue Squad boss surveyed the situation and allowed as how it was very likely that in order to extract Borden's hand from the disposer, "they might have to peel off his skin like a rubber glove." That, he estimated, would be the easy way out; he had heard of a man losing his entire hand in a similar situation.

I asked him: "Is there some way of shearing through the stainless steel to loosen the disposer?" He replied that this was a small town with no facilities for anything like that. I told him that I had read about something called the "Jaws of Life" that could shear through cars. He proceeded to phone an adjacent town and he did indeed locate the "Jaws of Life". A helmet was placed on Borden's head and the rescuers sheared through the body of the sink.

We were faced now with one little problem. Borden was still attached to a disposer the size of a healthy two-year-old baby. But at least now, Borden—released from the sink—could sit at the kitchen table during deliberations re the next move.

It was decided, unanimously, that nothing further could be done on the premises, and that the next move for Borden was a trip to the local hospital. In what turned out to be a fortunate hitch, we were told that the closest hospital was filled to capacity and that our caravan would have to drive a half-hour or so to the next closest hospital.

During Borden's ambulance ride, a young Rescue Squad volunteer, unbeknownst to the rest of us, had thought to take along a bag of ice. Throughout the entire trip to the hospital, she sat beside Borden, feeding ice into the opening between the disposer and Borden's arm. Just as we approached the hospital, his hand slipped out of the disposer.

Borden was treated for cuts and muscle strain and released at three in the morning. I know that you are on tenterhooks, waiting to learn about the tryst itself. I am happy to share.

We retired to our assigned bedroom. Borden's arm was in a sling. When we lay down, I looked straight ahead, facing the dresser. On the dresser, facing <u>me</u>, was a sculpture of the Blessed Mother. We wished each other good night.

Epilogue

My Secret

As we speak here, I am eighty-two-and-a-half years old, and to tell you the truth, I've held up pretty well. I think my marbles are all intact (My daughters would be the first to let me know if they weren't.) and most days, not too much hurts. Also, if I say so myself, I look pretty good for an old broad. This, all by way of working up to The Question:

"What is your Secret?"

I hear it a lot—mostly from younger women—and of course, I am flattered. Flattered, and delighted to share some of the life-lessons I have collected while trekking through this bumpy road from Mama's tummy to who-knows-where?

I think that the most important lesson I've learned is that every single one of us has a story—the story of a life—each with its unique balance of tragedy, comedy, sadness, happiness and mostly, just ordinariness.

I am convinced that how you hold up under your story pretty much determines the course and, even sometimes, the length of your life. It is no cliche to say that stress can kill. No longer a cliche because science has demonstrated that every fiber of our bodies is affected by stress—that an inordinate number of illnesses—resistant to traditional therapy—are actually stress-related, and disappear when the source of stress (or the mind-set) has changed.

My most important life lesson? For all of the stress-triggers that you feel helpless to cast aside, step back and weigh them in the scheme of things. I saw a paraplegic laughing as he listened to a little joke and I saw a woman who lives a life of luxury, crying over a broken fingernail.

Learn to handle stress.

My husband's death a few years ago, made me realize something I had never thought much about. Until Herb died, there had never been a time in my life when I wasn't Number One in someone's life: the daughter of my parents, the sister of my brothers, the wife of my husband. Now, I could leave my home and nobody knew or cared about my purpose or destination. That new experience is shared by most newly widowed men and women, from what I hear.

So, there is something else I've learned in my old age: it's important to be Number One in somebody's life. Of course, the ideal would be to have, or to find anew, a soul mate—-but, there are young people out there who need mentors, there are lonely patients confined to hospital beds, there are neighbors aching for company.

To sum it up, Mama's platitudes actually ring true: To have a friend, be a friend. Connect with the world....

I could go on forever because I am so high on life; check out my website once in a while where we can continue this dialog.

For now, I urge you: Have A Good Life!

*"If you don't learn to laugh
at trouble,
you won't have anything
to laugh at when you are old."*

Anonymous

Take A Sneak Peek at Glor's Next Book:

HOW TO REPAIR YOUR LIFE
A Tool Kit for the Social Screw-Up

by
Gloria Krasnow Liebenson

Contact Glor:
glor15@juno.com

978-0-595-35997-4
0-595-35997-3

Printed in the United States
34492LVS00006B/136-1008

9 780595 359974